JIMMY SCROGGI[NS]
WITH LESLEE BENNE[TT]

3 CIRCLES
GOSPEL CONVERSATIONS FOR LIFE

LifeWay Press®
Nashville, Tennessee

EDITORIAL TEAM, STUDENT MINISTRY PUBLISHING

Ben Trueblood
Director, Student Ministry

John Paul Basham
Manager, Student
Ministry Publishing

Karen Daniel
Editorial Team Leader

Andy McLean
Content Editor

Jennifer Siao
Production Editor

Sarah Sperry
Graphic Designer

ISBN: 978-1-5359-9882-6
Item Number: 005823084

Dewey Decimal Classification Number: 242.2
Subject Heading: DEVOTIONAL LITERATURE / BIBLE STUDY AND TEACHING / GOD

Printed in the United States of America

Student Ministry Publishing
LifeWay Resources
One LifeWay Plaza
Nashville, TN 37234-0144

We believe that the Bible has God for its author; salvation for its end; and truth, without any mixture of error, for its matter and that all Scripture is totally true and trustworthy. To review LifeWay's doctrinal guideline, please visit www.lifeway.com/doctrinalguideline.

TABLE OF CONTENTS

ABOUT THE AUTHORS

JIMMY SCROGGINS is the Lead Pastor of Family Church, where he has served since July 2008. He and his wife, Kristin, have eight children —James (Reilly), Daniel (Mary-Madison), Jeremiah, Isaac, Stephen, Anna Kate, Mary Claire, and Caleb. Under Jimmy's leadership, Family Church has grown to a network of 12 neighborhood churches— nine in English, two in Spanish and one in Portuguese. Family Church is passionate about building families by helping them discover and pursue God's design while carrying out their vision of taking the gospel to every person, in every family and neighborhood in South Florida. Jimmy is the coauthor of *Turning Everyday Conversations into Gospel Conversations* and hosts the Church for the Rest of Us podcast at familychurchnetwork.com. He also serves on the Board of LifeWay Christian Resources and is a member of the Board of Trustees at Palm Beach Atlantic University. Dr. Scroggins teaches as a visiting professor at both Southern and Southeastern Baptist Theological Seminaries.

LESLEE BENNETT

Leslee Bennett is the Communications Director at Family Church, where she has served since April 2013. She and her husband, George, have three children—Paige, Sam (Courtney), and Max. Prior to coming to Family Church, Leslee taught and led Community Bible Study of the Palm Beaches. Leslee is passionate about teaching the Bible and helping others know God's Word and live it out. She helped write *Turning Everyday Conversations into Gospel Conversations* and cohosts the Church for the Rest of Us podcast at familychurchnetwork.com. Early in her career, Leslee served as a speech writer in Washington, D.C. She is a graduate of Westmont College in Santa Barbara, CA, and is working on a master's in theological studies at The Southern Baptist Theological Seminary.

HOW TO USE

This Bible-study book provides six weeks of content for group and personal study. Each group session includes the following format to help facilitate meaningful dialogue and interaction during group time.

START

Every session contains an introduction to that week's session material, allowing for a natural transition into the biblical content for that week.

WATCH

Each session has a corresponding video to help explain the biblical content. Allow students to write down any notes and questions that may arise from the video and discuss them together before moving to the Discuss section.

DISCUSS

After watching the video, continue the study by moving to the Discuss section and working through the content provided there. The content in this section will expand on what was introduced in the video, offering depth and clarity to the biblical concepts being discussed.

APPLY

Following the Discuss section is the application section, allowing students the opportunity to work through the section of the 3 Circles diagram they just learned about.

PERSONAL STUDY

Each session provides three days of personal study, allowing students the opportunity to move deeper into the session material. With biblical teaching and questions for application, these sections challenge students to grow in their understanding of God's Word and to respond in faith.

INTRODUCTION

Three Circles is a tool to help us understand life and discover our God-given purpose. It is a way to think about life from a Christian perspective. It is a way to talk about life and the hope we have because of the gospel of Jesus. The three realities and three choices pictured on the next page are a way to process life as we know it.

This study will look at how this pattern plays out again and again through the lives of people in the Bible. We will also consider how it plays out again and again over the course of our lives.

The important fact to remember is that God is not asking us to always get it right; He is asking us to repent and keep on repenting. God is asking us to believe and keep on believing. No matter how many times we mess up, God is always offering us a way to recover and pursue His design for our lives.

REALITY #1   GOD'S DESIGN

God has a design for every aspect of our lives, and if we live according to God's design, then we have the opportunity to live in the arena of God's blessing. That is not to say that pursuing God's design exempts us from problems or difficult circumstances. But it is true that living life according to God's design is a better way to live than the alternatives.

CHOICE #1   SIN

God gave mankind a choice: to love God and live according to His design or do life our own way. When we do life our own way, the Bible calls this sin. Our choice is to sin or not to sin—to follow God's design or to pursue alternatives. The Bible points out that every one of us has sinned. We have a built-in tendency to violate God's design.

REALITY #2   BROKENNESS

When we operate our lives in ways that are contrary to God's design, we end up in the reality of brokenness. When something is broken it doesn't work the way it is supposed to work. A sinful life is a broken life. It isn't life the way God designed life to be. All of us have experienced brokenness and the awareness of our brokenness opens us up to the possibility of change.

CHOICE #2   REPENT & BELIEVE

Instead of trying to fix our own brokenness, which inevitably leads to failure and discouragement, the Bible offers us the solution as to where lasting change is found. The Bible explains that ultimate change comes about when we turn away from the sin that created the brokenness we feel, and we turn towards Jesus who can forgive our sins and heal the broken places in our lives. According to the Bible, repentance and belief (faith) go hand in hand. We turn from sin (repentance), and we turn to Jesus believing He can heal our brokenness.

REALITY #3   GOSPEL

The gospel is the only solution to our brokenness. The gospel is simply this: Jesus died on the cross for our sins, He was buried, and God raised Him from the dead (1 Cor. 15:3-4). Every person is invited to repent and believe the gospel. If they do, they will be forgiven for all of their sins, Jesus will come into their hearts, and He will begin to heal the broken places in their lives. The Bible also promises that everyone who believes the gospel will have a home in heaven.

CHOICE #3   RECOVER & PURSUE

From the moment we believe the gospel, God gives us the power to recover and pursue His design for our lives. God does not change our past, He does not always change painful circumstances, and He does not always remove difficult consequences of our sinful choices. God does make a way for us to be reconciled to Him through the gospel (2 Cor. 5:21). We have the opportunity to recover and pursue God's design from where we are "right now." Some parts of our lives may be healed immediately, some may be healed over time, still others may not be healed until we get to heaven. But whatever the case, we find that pursuing God's design is a better way to live.

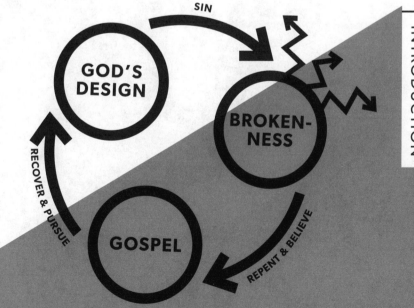

GOD'S DESIGN

START

Our study starts with the reality that God has a design. In fact, we can clearly see from Genesis 1-2 that He has a design for all of creation. He created all things on purpose and for a purpose.

> **What was the last item you purchased that came with instructions? Did you read the instructions, take a quick glance at the pictures, or toss the instructions aside? Explain.**

> **Is there any difference between the instructions for a simple Lego® set and the instructions on how to rebuild a diesel engine? If so, what is different?**

> **What are some things with sets of instructions where not consulting them would be disastrous?**

Some of us may wish for a detailed set of instructions on each aspect of our lives, no matter how small. But the truth is, our lives don't come with a detailed, step-by-step set of instructions. However, there is a manual—a set of instructions for how to live and relate to God and others. It explains God's purpose and design in creating us. It isn't simple like Lego instructions. Instead, it is more like that of the diesel engine—more involved and complex. But why shouldn't it be? We are, after all, complex persons who live in a complex world involved in complex relationships. Yet, God has not left us in the dark. God has a purpose and design for each of us, and that purpose and design is discovered through His Word.

WATCH

Watch the video "God's Design," before transitioning to the Discuss section.

DISCUSS

GOD'S DESIGN FOR ADAM AND EVE

Read Genesis 2:7-8,15-18,24-25.

What do these verses tell us about the kind of relationship God originally designed for us to have with Him?

What was God's design for how Adam and Eve would relate to each other?

God interacted directly with Adam and Eve. He literally formed them with His hands. He talked to them. He even gave them jobs. He instructed Adam to work the garden of Eden and watch over everything in it. God wanted to have a close, personal relationship with Adam and Eve with no shame and no fear of rejection.

Likewise, Adam and Eve were made specifically for one another. They were alike and yet different. They were attracted to one another. They were immediately committed to one another. They were designed to have a close, personal relationship with no shame and no fear of rejection, providing the model for all future human relationships. Their lifelong union and commitment to one another, as well as their fellowship and intimacy with God, was a big part of God's plan and design for them. The first couple would face a choice.

TO SIN OR NOT TO SIN

Read Genesis 3:1-6.

What were God's instructions to Adam and Eve? (Look back at Gen. 2:16-17.)

Have you ever chosen to sin even though you knew you were violating God's design? How did you rationalize your decision to go against His design?

Satan, in the form of a serpent, tempted Eve to doubt the goodness of God. Adam failed to intervene in the serpent's deception, and Eve encouraged him to eat the forbidden fruit like she did. In this series of choices, Adam and Eve violated God's design. They violated the relationship they were designed to have with God because they disobeyed His clear and loving instructions. They violated the relationship they had with one another because they failed to treat one another with trust, integrity, and honor. Finally, they violated the design for their relationship with creation because they ate from the tree that was forbidden to them. This series of sinful choices led to a series of painful consequences.

REALITY #2   ADAM AND EVE'S BROKENNESS

Brokenness is something with which we can all identify. Brokenness feels like guilt, shame, and regret. Brokenness hurts. If you have ever had a broken bone, you know that it hurts until it can be set right and begin to heal. If you have ever had a broken relationship, you know that it hurts until the relationship can be made right again. We experience brokenness when we sin and when others sin against us. Brokenness is a byproduct and a result of sinful choices.

Read Genesis 3:7-13.

Based on these verses, how did Adam and Eve react when they realized they had sinned?

What words or feelings would you associate with the brokenness you have personally experienced?

The story of the first sin is what theologians call "the fall." It is the moment when humans made the choice to disobey God. It is the moment when sin entered the world and distorted our relationship with our Creator. Instead of relating to God directly and intimately, Adam and Eve hid from God and were afraid of Him. Instead of honoring and trusting one another, Adam and Eve blamed one another. And for the first time, they were ashamed to be naked. Instead of relationships characterized by love and trust, the relationships in the story became full of fear and suspicion. Everything that was once declared good has now been broken. God responded by pronouncing a curse on the serpent and on mankind (Read also Gen. 3:14-20). Our relationship to God is broken but it isn't broken beyond repair. God made a way back to Him. It is a way foreshadowed in the Old Testament and fulfilled in the New Testament through the person and work of Jesus.

Read Genesis 3:15.

This is the first place the Bible points to the coming of Jesus. God is speaking to the serpent, who is Satan, about the "seed of the woman," who is Jesus. Satan will motivate people to crucify Jesus, yet it is through His death, burial, and resurrection that Jesus will crush Satan forever.

CHOICE #2 · *FIXING ADAM AND EVE'S BROKENNESS*

Remember back to how Adam and Eve felt shame in Genesis 3:7. Adam and Eve saw their nakedness, felt shame, and sewed fig leaves together to cover themselves. This was man's first attempt to fix his own brokenness.

What are some ways people today try to cover their guilt, shame, and regret?

REALITY #3 · *GOD COVERS ADAM AND EVE'S SIN*

Read Genesis 3:21.

The fig leaves weren't adequate to cover Adam and Eve's sin. The change, forgiveness, and healing they were looking for required something much more painful. Someone had to die in order to make things right (see Gen. 2:16-17). But God, in His mercy, allowed an animal sacrifice in the place of the physical death of Adam and Eve.

How does this foreshadow what we know about Jesus' death on the cross (see also Matt. 26:26-28; Heb. 9:22)?

CHOICE #3 · *ADAM AND EVE RECOVER & PURSUE GOD'S DESIGN*

Adam and Eve sinned, and their sin had consequences. It had consequences for them and for all of humankind for all time. Yet God is a gracious, merciful, and compassionate. He made a way forward for them. Adam and Eve had to leave the garden, but they and all of their descendants (including us) are still able to recover and pursue His design for their lives.

Read Genesis 3:22–4:2.

How did Adam and Eve recover and pursue God's design for:

- **Their relationship with God (see also Gen. 3:21)?**

- **Their relationship with each other (Gen. 4:1)?**

- **Their relationship to creation (Gen. 4:2)?**

God took the initiative to cover Adam and Eve's sin in a way that allowed them to reestablish their relationship with Him. God still allowed them to be fruitful and multiply by giving them many children (Gen. 5:4). God allowed them to work the ground and care for the animals. Although they were forgiven and God began to heal their brokenness, their sinful choices still had serious and lasting consequences. After the fall, everything became more difficult for Adam and Eve and all of humankind. It is only because of God's love and mercy that we are able to recover and pursue God's design.

What are some ways you see God's design coming together in your life?

APPLY

Fill out this diagram with the three realities and three choices mentioned on page 7.

Partner up and practice explaining the concept of God's design to your partner. (You might want to start with: I have come to believe that God has a purpose and design for our lives.)

GOD'S DESIGN FOR YOU

We've seen how God had a design for all of creation. Out of nothing, He created everything. God created the heavens and the earth. He created the sun, moon, and all the stars. He created every living creature. When you stop to ponder the vast number and wide variety of God's creative acts, it's easy to think that God is too far away and far too busy to be concerned about you. Then we read the following Psalm penned by King David as he pondered God and His relationship to His people.

Read Psalm 139:13-16.

Knitting is a bit of a lost art. It requires meticulous attention to detail and laser focus on the part of one doing the knitting. Here, David draws an analogy to how God knits us together, making us into the exact person He wants us to be.

> **Circle the words (verbs) in Psalm 139:13-16 that describe God's intentionality in creating each person and write them here:**
>
> **Verse 13 _____ and _____**
>
> **Verse 14 _____**
>
> **Verse 15 _____ and _____**

Read Psalm 139:16.

> *"Your eyes saw me when I was formless;*
> *all my days were written in your book and*
> *planned before a single one of them began."*

We see how God created, knit, made, and formed us in advance to do all He planned for us to do. Eric Liddell understood this. Raised by missionaries in China, Liddell evacuated to Scotland when he was just boy. He grew up to be a great runner who won a gold medal in the 1924 Olympics. In the Oscar-award winning movie, *Chariots of Fire*, Liddell says this to his sister who is begging him to go back to China to continue their parents' mission work: "I've decided. I'm going back to China … but I've got a lot of running to do first. Jen, Jen, you've got to understand. I believe that God made me for a purpose, for China, but He also made me fast and when I run, I feel His pleasure. To give it up would be to hold Him in contempt. You were right. It's not just fun; to win is to honor Him."[1] Liddell knew God designed him to run and he knew that God had plans for him. The same is true for you. God designed you and He has plans for you.

CHALLENGE OF THE DAY

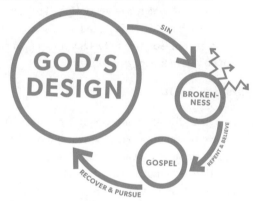

Focus on God's design for you. What are some of the ways He uniquely designed you?

• **Physical**

• **Personality**

• **Talents and Gifts**

How do you see God using your unique design right now?

Does your unique design give you any hints about ways that God could use you in the future?

GOD HAS PLANS FOR YOU

If you come across a watch laying on the ground, you instinctively know that the watch is not just a random, natural collection of springs and gears. In other words, you know it didn't just come into being from nothing or by chance. When you see a watch, you know it has been designed. Moreover, you know it was designed to do something—tell time. In addition to fulfilling its purpose, watches are also made for style. They are made out of certain materials to look a certain way and make a particular statement. A watch is never designed or assembled on accident. A watch is always designed and assembled for a purpose. So were you! God had to teach a young man named Jeremiah that he was made for a purpose.

Read Jeremiah 1:5-10.

Jeremiah was an Old Testament prophet. He lived 600 years before Jesus. He preached against the worship of false gods. Jeremiah was such a strong preacher that other prophets came against him and tried to shut him down. There must have been times when Jeremiah doubted whether or not he was the right person for God to use in this way. Jeremiah felt like he was too young and inexperienced to do big things for God. God made it clear to Jeremiah that he was doing what God created him to do.

God said something similar to the apostle Paul in the New Testament:

> *"But when God, who from my mother's womb set me apart and called me by his grace, was pleased to reveal his Son in me, so that I could preach him among the Gentiles..."* ***(Gal. 1:15-16a)***

16 | 3 CIRCLES

Paul knew that he was called from his mother's womb to preach the gospel. That truth must have encouraged Paul when he felt inadequate or when his message was not well received. You might be surprised to know that if you are a believer, God says something similar about you. He says:

> *"For you are saved by grace through faith, and this is not from yourselves; it is God's gift—not from works, so that no one can boast. For we are his workmanship, created in Christ Jesus for good works, which God prepared ahead of time for us to do"* ***(Eph. 2:8-10).***

According to verse 10, why are you "created in Christ Jesus"?

When did God determine the work you are supposed to do?

CHALLENGE OF THE DAY

If you could only finish this sentence with one thing, what would it be? I am created in Christ Jesus to _____.

Talk to a parent, teacher, coach, or mentor and ask them what ways God has uniquely designed you. Ask them how they see God using your unique design in the lives of others.

17 | GOD'S DESIGN

GOD BELIEVES IN YOU

Many people struggle to believe that God has designed them for important purposes. This struggle is especially difficult for students who are in middle school, high school, and college. There are plenty of reasons for many of us to see ourselves as inadequate or unworthy for God's purposes. Some of us struggle with comparing ourselves to others. We see other people who are better looking or more talented or more popular, or who just seem to have it more together than we do. Some of us struggle because we have been criticized or belittled. Whatever the case, many people struggle to believe that God actually loves them, believes in them, and created them for a purpose.

Joseph is a character in the Bible who had many reasons to struggle with confidence in God. You can read his life story in Genesis 37-50. Joseph was belittled and criticized by his older brothers. His relationship with his brothers deteriorated to the point that they kidnapped him, faked his death, and sold him into slavery in another country. As a slave, he was falsely accused of sexual assault and thrown into prison. In prison, he was forgotten and betrayed by people who owed him favors. Even after Joseph was released from prison and elevated to an important political position in Egypt, he still had to operate in a corrupt system and under the heavy influence of a false religion. But instead of allowing criticism, false accusations, betrayal, isolation, and loneliness to shake his confidence in God, Joseph believed that God was at work through it all. And He was.

In *Toy Story 4*, Bonnie's first day of kindergarten is very difficult. She doesn't connect with the other kids and she ends up sitting at a table by herself, isolated and lonely. Given the opportunity to make a craft, Bonnie reaches into the trash can, pulls out a spork, and makes a doll from the spork, using googly eyes, pipe cleaners, and pieces of a tongue depressor. She names her new doll Forky. She immediately loves Forky and wants Forky to be with her at all times. Forky, however, doesn't understand Bonnie's affection for him nor Bonnie's desire to have a friendship with him. Throughout the movie, Forky is always trying to get away from Bonnie and get back into the trash can. In one of the most poignant lines of the movie, Forky says, "I'm not a toy, I was made for soups, salads, maybe chili, and then the trash."[2] Through all of the adventures portrayed in *Toy Story 4*, Forky is eventually persuaded that Bonnie loves him and wants him. He begins to believe that he's not trash after all. The reason this element of the movie resonates is because so many people have similar thoughts about themselves. They think, "I can't be significant, valuable, or purposeful because I am inadequate or unworthy." Believers in Jesus need to remember that through the gospel we have been made worthy and we have been given a purpose. God made us and He wants a relationship with us. Awareness of this truth should give us confidence to pursue the purposes for which God created us.

CHALLENGE OF THE DAY

Look up the following verses as you seek to combat the following struggles or feelings.

- **Inadequacy: Philippians 4:13**

- **Unworthiness: Hebrews 4:15-16**

- **Comparing myself to others: Galatians 1:10**

- **Criticism: 1 Peter 2:23**

- **Fear of failure: Isaiah 41:10**

19

GOD'S DESIGN

SIN

START

Have you ever noticed that there is a tendency inside of you to push back against authority? Nobody likes to be bossed around. Even when those giving us instructions are people who generally love us—like family, friends, teachers, or pastors—there is something inside of us that thinks we know better.

Of course, this tendency is not all bad. After all, God wants us to exercise leadership, and sometimes exercising leadership means challenging the process. At its best, this tendency makes us do what God designed us to do. However, at its worst, our capacity for doing things our own way can be very wrong. God has given us a design for our lives and when we choose to depart from God's design the Bible says we are living in sin.

The Bible has a number of different words for sin—iniquity, transgression, rebellion. In its simplest form, sin is defined as missing the mark. It is missing the mark of God's standard that is based on His character. It is failing to bring Him glory in the things we do.

While our culture may not like to use the language of personal sin and call it out when they see it, the Bible doesn't tip-toe around the issue. There is a reason for the break away from God's design and a reason for the brokenness we see around us each day—and that reason is sin.

WATCH

Watch the video "Sin," before transitioning to the Discuss section.

DISCUSS

GOD'S DESIGN FOR DAVID

God had a design for the way David was to exercise leadership in his nation, in his family, and in his personal conduct. In this story, David failed in all three arenas. He failed as a national leader. He failed as the leader of his family. And he failed to lead himself. David departed from God's design and then he—and others around him—had to deal with the consequences.

CHOICE #1 **DAVID'S SIN**

In 2 Samuel 11, we read the story of David's most famous failure—his affair with a woman named Bathsheba.

Read 2 Samuel 11:1-5.

So, where did David mess up? For starters, David chose to neglect his responsibilities. It was the king's job to lead his army into war during the springtime. Historians tell us that battles between warring peoples stopped for the winter and resumed when the weather improved in the spring.[1] David should have been leading his army to battle rather than lounging on his roof. He should have been looking after his men rather than lusting after Bathsheba. David's failure to focus on his responsibilities created space for temptation.

We have the potential to fall into the same pattern as David. Jobs, school, church, sports, choir, band, and so on, give us responsibilities that keep our eyes on productive activities. When we avoid or neglect responsibility, we create space in our lives for temptation and can easily be led into sin.

In what ways have you opened the door for temptation by neglecting responsibility in your own life?

One thing we can learn from David's sin is to not place ourselves in areas of life that will naturally lead to temptation.

What are those areas or places where you could be vulnerable to temptation? How can you avoid putting yourself in those places?

The second thing David did was he entertained his temptation instead of turning away when he saw Bathsheba bathing. Sometimes, we entertain our sin by thinking that as long as we don't go too far it isn't wrong. But sin begins in the heart and makes its way into our actions. If we don't stop the sinful temptation at its source, it will eventually make its way into our lives.

What are some strategies that you could use when you find yourself tempted to entertain a personal sin?

Finally, David gave into temptation and chose to sin. After inquiring about Bathsheba, David proceeded to send for her so that he could sleep with her. This was an intentional act of disobedience, rejecting God's design in favor of pursuing his own selfish pleasure. In fact, one of the things about sin is that it tempts us to believe that God's design is actually keeping something good from us. Sin would have us believe that if we do things our own way, we will be happier, we will have more fun, and we will experience greater satisfaction. Sin tries to make God's design look restrictive and causes us to wonder if God really has our best interests in mind.

Why do we often underestimate the power sin can have in our lives if left unchecked?

REALITY #2 DAVID'S BROKENNESS

Sin has consequences. Some consequences are immediate. Some don't appear until much later. We don't know how much time elapsed between verses 4 and 5 of 2 Samuel 11, but the consequences of David's sin were significant. Bathsheba sent word back to the palace that she was pregnant. David's private sin was about to become a very public sin. He was going to be embarrassed in front of his family, his friends, and his nation. The reality is that our sin is never hidden. We may be able to hide it from other people, but the Bible tells us that all sin is against God and that He sees all.

Describe a time you made a huge mistake, tried to cover it up, and realized that you weren't going to be able to keep it a secret.

CHOICE #2 DAVID TRIED TO FIX HIS BROKENNESS

David knew he was in trouble. His first instinct was to try to fix it himself. Instead of taking the difficult path of making things right, owning his sin, turning to God, or turning to others for wise counsel, David tried to clean up the mess and instead he made it a lot worse.

Read 2 Samuel 11:6-14.

David's refusal to deal directly with his sin motivated him to dig the hole even deeper. He increased his sin and deceit by trying to "fix" the situation. First, he tried to hide his sin by calling Bathsheba's husband home from the war and giving them opportunity to sleep together. When that didn't work, he got Uriah drunk and tried again. When that failed, he successfully arranged to have Uriah killed in battle. A number of unnamed warriors were killed as well. By trying to cover up his own sin, David actually compounded his sins, which brought hurt and pain upon other individuals and their families.

How have you seen sin draw you or someone else into further sinning?

How have you seen sin and its consequences affect those around the person sinning?

REALITY #3   *GOD FORGAVE DAVID'S SIN*

David thought he got away with it. He covered up the affair, married Bathsheba, and they had a son. His plan worked—or so he thought. In 2 Samuel 12, God sent the prophet Nathan to confront David. To David's credit, he owned up to his sin and expressed genuine repentance (v. 13). Once David confessed his sin, God forgave him.

Do you feel like David's sins were too great to be forgiven? Have you ever felt as if your sins were beyond God's willingness or ability to forgive?

David's sins were significant and severe. And even though God forgave him, David still had to face painful consequences. The firstborn son of David and Bathsheba got sick and died. David's family was a mess for the rest of his life. His children constantly fought with one another. David's personal relationships were often very difficult. One of his sons even tried to kill him. God's forgiveness does not exempt us from consequences. Even through painful consequences, God continued to be with David and used him to bring about His promises of redemption.

CHOICE #3   *DAVID RECOVERED & PURSUED GOD'S DESIGN*

Read Psalm 51:4-12.

In this Psalm, David expressed his desire to recover and pursue God's design. He asked God to change him from the inside out. He didn't make excuses for his sin. He didn't justify his sin, nor did he minimize his sin. Instead, David confessed his sin and appealed to the mercy of God as his only hope.

What parts of David's confession stand out to you? What parts can you easily identify with?

APPLY

Fill out this diagram with the three realities and three choices mentioned on page 7.

Take the last few minutes of time today to practice sharing the 3 Circles with one another. Take special care to define sin based on what you learned today.

THE STRUGGLE IS REAL

Just because we're forgiven doesn't mean we're exempt from struggle with sin. In this week's group Bible study, we saw how one of the Bible's greatest heroes, King David, struggled with sin. We know that God calls David "a man after my own heart" (Acts 13:22), yet David messed up over and over again. The truth is we all mess up over and over again. Paul—another one of the greatest Bible heroes—described the believer's struggle with sin.

Read Romans 7:14-24.

According to verse 18, Paul desired to do
_____.

According to verse 19, Paul practiced the
_____ that he does not want to do.

List some of the ways your struggle with sin mirrors Paul's.

In Romans 7:24, Paul asked a rhetorical question: "Who will rescue me?" Paul acknowledged that the struggle is real but there is a way forward. Throughout the Book of Romans, Paul presents Jesus as the only hope for salvation from sin. He also tells us how the Holy Spirit helps us fight the battle against sin.

Read Romans 8:26.

We are never alone in our struggle with sin. We can choose to do good with the help of the Holy Spirit and encouragement from other believers. God doesn't want us to struggle alone.

CHALLENGE OF THE DAY

Ask the Holy Spirit right now to help you in your struggle with sin.

Who are some friends who encourage you in your battle against sin?

Is there a godly adult in your life who could help you with strategies to battle against specific areas of temptation you're facing?

Talk to these people this week and ask them to pray for you.

THE PRACTICE OF CONFESSION

One cold and snowy day in February, two math majors at Reid College in Oregon built a giant snowball at the top of the hill and gave it a shove. The snowball gathered speed and size as it catapulted down the hill smashing into a dorm building, ultimately causing $3,000 worth of damage.[2] They seriously miscalculated the damage a snowball could do to the building below.

Sin, when we try to manage it on our own, snowballs. It leads us into more and more sin. The snowball gets bigger and bigger to the point where it's completely out of control. We saw that with David. His sin multiplied the more he tried to cover it up. David went from looking on a woman with lust to coveting his neighbor's wife to committing adultery to lying to ultimately committing murder. We can be guilty of doing this as well.

How can you stop the snowball? The answer is in turning from your own sin through confession and repentance. Confession and repentance go hand-in-hand. Repentance is when we turn away from our sin and toward God. Confession is when we agree with God that we have violated His design and ask for His undeserved mercy.

Read Psalm 51:4-10.

Notice what David learned about sin in verse 4: all sin is against God and God alone. David was far from perfect and in the New Testament God calls him "a man after my own heart" (Acts 13:22). What made David a man after God's heart wasn't his perfect living, but rather his life of repentance. David was a really good repenter. He fell down but he got back up with the help of the Holy Spirit and other committed believers. True repentance is always accompanied by true confession.

The key to confession is taking personal responsibility for your own heart and your own actions.

> **Go through Psalm 51 and circle any form of the words *sin*, *guilt*, and *rebellion*. David took full ownership for his own sinful choices.**

David knew that God's response to confession is always mercy and forgiveness.

> **Now go back through Psalm 51 and underline places where you see the words *purify*, *wash*, and *clean*.**

CHALLENGE OF THE DAY

> **Draw the 3 Circles (see page 7) focusing on the sin that has separated or is separating you from God right now.**

Think about the brokenness you have experienced in your life. Now, remind yourself of the gospel. Jesus died on the cross for your sins. He was buried. God raised Him from the dead. If you have repented and confessed your sins, then your sins are forgiven in Christ. You can recover and pursue His design from right where you are. You can be a person after God's own heart, too!

HOPE FOR THE SINNER

Almost everyone has heard the story of Noah and the flood, but do you remember why God sent the flood?

Read Genesis 6:5-6.

The flood was God's judgment against the wickedness of humanity. When we violate God's design, we break the law of God. You could say that when we sin, we commit crimes against God Himself.

Now, when someone commits a crime, you have probably heard it said: "That person owes a debt to society." If he is caught and found guilty, he might pay a fine or do jail time (or worse, he could be executed.) In the same way, when we commit crimes against God we are guilty before God and we owe a debt to God for our crimes. Because of God's character as a holy and righteous judge, God can't simply sweep our crimes under the rug and pretend they never happened. The penalty must be paid.

When Jesus was crucified on the cross, He paid the penalty for the sins of the world. He paid the fine. He did the time. He was executed for crimes that He never personally committed. He died in our place for our sins.

The cross makes it possible for God to judge our sins by judging Jesus in our place, while simultaneously forgiving our sins because of the righteousness given to us by Christ.

Read Psalm 32.

David wrote these words 1,000 of years before Jesus was born. Jesus came to forgive the guilt of sinners—that's the good news.

When was the last time you rejoiced about being forgiven by Jesus? If it's been a while, pause right now and pray a prayer of praise.

In summary, we are all sinners. We miss the mark. We wander away and even reject God's perfect design. As a result, we all owe a tremendous debt. Jesus came to earth to pay our debt to God by dying for us on the cross. If you have received Jesus, your debt is paid and you can rejoice as David did.

CHALLENGE OF THE DAY

In this week's devotions, we looked at Romans 7, Psalm 51, and Psalm 32. Out of these passages, choose a verse or two that challenged you the most and post them on social media, briefly explaining why they were meaningful, and use #3Circles. You may want to start your post with something like, "I'm doing a Bible study with some friends and this week I read these verses." Post the verses. Then say, "These verses are important because …"

BROKEN-NESS

START

When you were younger you might have spent hours building something amazing with a Lego set, only for your design to be shattered by a younger sibling. Because you designed it and built it out of your own heart and with your own hands, you are the only one who could put it back together. Even if they tried, your younger sibling could never reconstruct your creation. If it was up to them, your Lego design would be broken forever. But because you are the designer, you have the ability to rebuild what has been broken.

God has a design for every part of life, no matter how big or how small. When sin causes us to depart from that design we end up in the reality of brokenness. This uncomfortable reality turns God's masterful design into something that resembles a broken Lego set. God has a design for marriage, yet we see divorce rampant in our culture. God has a design for finances, yet we live in a world filled with debt. God has a design for friendship, yet we live in a world filled with conflict. We live in a world filled with brokenness. Brokenness is the byproduct of sin. It is the consequence of our personal sin, the sin of others, and the sin that surrounds us in a broken world.

Have you ever spent a long time building something only for it to break? How did it break? How did you react?

What are some aspects of God's good creation that you see broken around you today?

WATCH

Watch the video "Brokenness," before transitioning to the Discuss section.

DISCUSS

Let's look at the interaction Jesus had with the woman at the well in John 4 and see how sin led her to brokenness. In this story, we see how Jesus restored her, and enabled her to recover and pursue God's good design for her life.

REALITY #1   *GOD'S DESIGN FOR THE WOMAN*

Read John 4:4-10.

According to verse 10:

- **What did Jesus want to give the woman?**

- **What are two things she needed to know to get the living water?**

The woman only saw things from an earthly perspective, but Jesus knew she needed more than water from a well. She needed to see that God wanted a relationship with her. She was alone during the hottest part of the day drawing water. Typically, women would come to the well in the cool of the day. It was their opportunity to do their work while socializing with one another.

CHOICE #1   *THE WOMAN'S SIN*

Read John 4:11-18.

This woman didn't want to see other people, which is why she went to the well when most people typically didn't go. Her sordid past and her soiled reputation preceded her. Her guilt, shame, and brokenness motivated her to hide. She didn't want to be seen. She was a lonely and broken woman, but God had more for her. He had a plan to pull her in, lift her up, and send her out to tell others about Jesus, the living water.

Have you or someone you know made choices that hurt your reputation?

Why might it be difficult for someone to repair his/her reputation?

Jesus talked about water that would ensure the woman never thirsted again. She was intrigued by the thought of avoiding more humiliating trips to the well. The woman, however, was only thinking about her physical needs. Jesus was speaking to her spiritual need. He got her attention by bringing up her broken past and the difficulty of her present situation. He told her that He knew about her five husbands and that the man she was currently living with was not her husband. We don't know if all of those relationships ended in death or divorce. Either way, the woman was seen as damaged goods. Sin had impacted her life in a big way.

REALITY #2 — THE WOMAN'S BROKENNESS

Reread John 4:11-18.

It is possible—and maybe even likely—that the woman at the well had never known a healthy male-female relationship. Her brokenness went deep and had lasted a long time. We don't know the details, but we can imagine that this woman might have believed that men could not be trusted. She had very likely been hurt and used, and possibly even abused. It was a series of sinful choices, some of her own and probably some by others, that had set the trajectory of her present reality.

This woman was so broken that it affected the way she lived her daily life. She walked to the well alone in the middle of the day, dripping sweat, unlike the other women who all went together in the cool air of dawn. She was an outcast. She was lonely, ashamed, and despised.

How would you describe the brokenness you feel about the sin that you have personally committed?

How does this differ from the feeling of brokenness you have when someone sins against you?

Read John 4:19.

Jesus addressed her wounds. The woman tried to divert attention toward an age-old "theological" debate between the Samaritans (which she was) and the Jews (which Jesus was). The Jews were not fans of the Samaritans. From the viewpoint of an orthodox Jew like Jesus, this woman had three strikes against her: she was a Samaritan, a woman, and a sexual sinner.

Like the woman, when we are confronted with our brokenness and our sin, our first instinct is to try to explain it away, change the subject, or escape from our own broken feelings. Our sin makes us feel dirty, empty, worthless, and inadequate.

It is human nature to try to escape these feelings. For example, if we find ourselves in a broken relationship, we jump into a different relationship. Some people turn to drugs and alcohol to try to numb broken feelings. Others attempt to address their brokenness by working hard, making money, and diving into materialism. Some people try to deal with brokenness by becoming more religious, or expending tremendous effort to become a better person. All of these attempts ultimately fail because the changes brought about by these efforts don't go deep enough and don't last long enough. God allows us to experience brokenness to teach us that we cannot truly change ourselves.

CHOICE #2 THE WOMAN REPENTED & BELIEVED

Read John 4:21-29.

What did the woman do to demonstrate that she was changed by Jesus? (see John 4:28-29)?

Have you ever felt Jesus calling you to repent and believe? If so, what was that like?

Every day the woman carried her water jar to the well. For her, the water jar was a symbol of her shame because she would rather carry it to the well in the heat of the day than have to face the disapproval of the other women in town. But when Jesus offered her living water, it was apparent that she received it by faith. She left her water jar behind so she could tell people about the living water that she had found. When Jesus invites us to repent, believe, and be forgiven, all of us have our own water jars to leave behind.

What "water jar" is Jesus calling you to leave behind?

REALITY #3 GOD COVERS THE WOMAN'S SIN

Reread John 4:25-26.

What was Jesus claiming?

What would Jesus eventually do to cover her sin?

CHOICE #3 THE WOMAN RECOVERED AND PURSUED GOD'S DESIGN

Read John 4:39-42.

What is the evidence that the woman recovered and pursued God's design (see again John 4:28-29)? How did God use her influence?

How does God want us to use our influence to point others to Him?

God used this woman's brokenness to bring others to Jesus. Her story was a powerful testimony for Christ in her town. Although the Bible doesn't give us any more information about the woman beyond what's contained in John 4, we can be sure that her life was never perfect or easy. But her new life in Christ was full of hope and purpose. She had been given the ministry of reconciliation.

APPLY

Fill out this diagram with the three realities and three choices mentioned on page 7.

Partner up and practice explaining the concept of brokenness to your partner. Share the feelings that brokenness has brought you and pray for one another.

ESCAPING THE BROKENNESS

Jesus spoke directly into the broken places in the life of the woman at the well. He pursued her heart by bringing both her dark past and present brokenness into the light. Have you ever been in your dark, cozy room only to have a family member turn the lights on? It's not pleasant! You want to escape the light, so you pull the covers over your head. This is what we often do when we're confronted by sin and brokenness. The woman at the well pulled the "theological debate" covers over her head in an attempt to take the focus off of her brokenness. We have all kinds of covers we pull over ourselves to hide from being exposed. They all look different, but they accomplish the same purpose. They shield us from the goodness of God's design and keep us in the dark.

Read John 4:13-20.

What are some ways you try to escape feelings of brokenness?

Below are some examples for you to think through. Mark any that relate to you, or note other ways you try to escape brokenness.

☐ **"I run back to sinful habits."**

☐ **"I try to become more religious."**

☐ **"I distract myself with alcohol, drugs, and partying."**

☐ **"I change the subject to something lighter."**

☐ **"I dive into romantic or sexual relationships."**

☐ **"I go to play sports or my hobby."**

Notice that some of these options are not wrong. It's not a sin for you to hang out with friends or play sports. Those are good things. But just like the woman at the well, we sometimes use a good thing to distract us from the ultimate thing.

CHALLENGE OF THE DAY

In the space provided, what are some areas of brokenness you have experienced?

Now, on the lines to the right, list some of the things you have done to escape those feelings.

Thank God for the ways He responds to the feelings you've experienced in your brokenness (example: "God, in my brokenness I've felt alone. Thank You for sending Your Son to show me that I will never be alone. You are with me.")

Then take time to confess to the Lord the ways you've tried to escape your brokenness apart from Him.

FIXING THE BROKENNESS

When something breaks, we want to fix it. When your phone breaks, you take it to the phone store. When your car breaks, you take it to the mechanic. When you break your arm, you go to the doctor. Broken things need to be fixed. This tendency to want to fix broken things is hardwired into us. It's easy for us to accept that the phone manufacturer is going to do the best job fixing our phone. The mechanic is trained to fix our car. The doctor is the only one who can fix our arm. Yet we struggle to believe that God is only one who can fix our heart.

David knew what it felt like to be broken by his own sins. Even as a hero of the faith, he repeatedly found himself in broken situations. But David developed an incredible capacity to respond to brokenness by turning to the Lord.

Read Psalm 6.

When you are feeling brokenness, it's normal to ask God questions about your circumstances. In verse 3, David asks God how long he's going to feel broken.

> **What kinds of questions have you wanted to ask God in response to brokenness?**

Some forms of brokenness last a long time. For example, if your parents get divorced, that's a reality you have to deal with the rest of your life. If someone is abused, that's a wound that becomes a permanent part of that person's story. Now, these things don't define a person or become their identity, but it is something that leaves an ugly mark on their lives. It's not something that God can't heal or restore; it's just that brokenness leaves scars. David reflected on his extended issues of brokenness in verses 4-7.

Are there issues of brokenness in your life that may last for an extended period?

David expressed confidence that God is loving and powerful. He declared that in spite of his feelings of brokenness and guilt and the sinfulness of his own choices, God still loved him, knew him, and He would answer his prayers. David brought his brokenness to God.

Has there ever been a time when you were able to take your brokenness to God? Would you be willing to do that right now?

CHALLENGE OF THE DAY

Find a mentor in your life or a pastor at your church and talk to them about the brokenness you are facing. It could be sin that you have committed or sin that's been committed against you. Tell them how it's made you feel broken, then ask them to pray for you and give you guidance moving forward.

NOTES

USING THE BROKENNESS

NOTES

A water bearer in India had two large pots—one hung on each end of a pole which she carried on her back. One of the pots had a crack in it and could only deliver half the water it was intended to provide. The perfect pot was proud of its accomplishments, while the cracked pot was ashamed of its imperfections.

The water bearer asked the cracked pot what was wrong. The cracked pot said, "You have to do all of this work, but because of all my flaws I don't give what the other pot offers." The water bearer pointed to the road they had been traveling on and asked, "Did you notice the flowers are only on your side, but not on the other pot's side? That's because I have always known about your flaw, and I've been using it to create a masterpiece. For two years I have been able to pick these beautiful flowers to decorate my table. Without you being just the way you are, I would not have this beauty to grace my house." The water bearer saw the beauty in the brokenness and used it to make something beautiful.[1]

God does this with us. We're all broken, and God wants to use our broken past to create something truly remarkable. Writing to the church in Corinth, Paul wanted them to see the brokenness around them just like the water bearer saw her cracked pot. The persecution they faced, and the harshness of the world would make a beautiful masterpiece in the right hands.

Read 2 Corinthians 4:7-10.

"This treasure" refers to the good news of Jesus Christ. God places His most prized possession in everyday clay jars called people—people who will get perplexed, persecuted, and knocked down. God uses the broken places in our lives to put His glory on display. Let's think about ways that God uses brokenness:

1. *The brokenness in your life is meant to point you to God.*
   The Bible tells us that Paul had a "thorn in the flesh."
   He pleaded with God to take the thorn away and God
   responded, "My grace is sufficient for you, for my power
   is perfected in weakness" (2 Cor. 12:9). Like Paul, what if
   God is using broken things in your life to draw you back to
   His sufficiency and grace?

2. *The brokenness in your life is meant to pull others in and lift
   them up.* The woman at the well left her water jar and ran
   back to her hometown telling everyone about Jesus. God
   used her brokenness for something amazing. Her story
   brought many people to faith in Jesus. Her brokenness
   was on full display and from her broken past God pieced
   together a beautiful masterpiece of change.

   **How do you think God wants to use your
   brokenness to help others?**

CHALLENGE OF THE DAY

Post a verse that has meant the most to you throughout the
devotions this week with #3Circles. Offer to pray for those
who are feeling broken.

NOTES

REPENT & BELIEVE

START

When something is broken, we have a choice to make—we can try to fix it ourselves or take it to someone who knows what they are doing. When we depart from God's design and end up in brokenness, we have a choice to make. We can try to fix it ourselves or we can choose to turn from our own ways and trust in God's way to provide healing.

The apostle Paul was a man who was really good at trying to fix himself. He was an extremely religious man who made it his business to follow all of God's rules and make sure others did too. He thought he was doing right until a dramatic encounter with Jesus changed everything. Paul changed his mind, his heart, and the direction of his life. He repented and believed.

To repent is to change. It is a change of mind that leads to a change of heart that leads to a change in behavior. To believe is to trust. Belief is more than educating ignorance and more than affirming something as true. Belief is trusting something or someone with your whole life.

WATCH

Watch the video "Repent and Believe," before transitioning to the Discuss section.

GROUP DISCUSSION

REALITY #1 GOD'S DESIGN FOR PAUL

The apostle Paul was frequently arrested for preaching about Jesus. On these occasions, Paul would use his interactions with prison guards, bureaucrats, and important officials to continue to talk about Jesus. In Acts 26, Paul testified on his own behalf in a trial before King Agrippa. Agrippa was an important and influential political leader in Paul's day.

Read Acts 26:1-5.

Based on these verses, how was Paul raised?

What does this tell us about how Paul viewed his relationship with God?

Paul was raised in a Jewish family. He was very familiar with God's design for all things, as described in Genesis 1-2. It was likely that Paul had memorized the first five books of the Old Testament (including the Book of Genesis) by the time he was twelve years old. In a letter he wrote to a group of Christians in Rome, Paul talked about how God's design is so evident in the intricacy of creation that no one—religious or not—can honestly deny it (Rom. 1:20). Paul thought his relationship with the Creator was totally dependent upon doing more good than bad. This is why Paul lived as a Pharisee, which meant he was a strict, rule-following religious person. Paul would quickly learn the sin problem was not one he could solve on his own.

CHOICE #1 PAUL'S LIFE BEFORE HE ENCOUNTERED CHRIST

Read Acts 26:6-9.

According to verse 9, what is the root of Paul's sin?

Jesus did not come to abolish the Jewish laws, but to fulfill them (Matt. 5:17). The entire Old Testament points to Jesus as the Savior of the world. Jesus was the key component of God's design from the very beginning. Paul, a dedicated Pharisee, made the personal choice to deny Jesus. Similar to David's adultery with Bathsheba, this was a sinful choice that Paul convinced himself to make over time. Paul wrote about how Adam's original sin cursed all of us with a sinful nature (Rom. 5:12). This sinful nature convinces each of us to sin and fall short of God's glory (Rom. 3:23). No matter how big or small the sin, you do not have to fall far to fall short. The sin problem is a universal one that none of us can solve on our own.

Read Acts 26:10-11.

Based on these verses, how did Paul try to resolve his own brokenness?

How have your attempts to resolve your brokenness ever pushed you into more sin and more brokenness?

Paul tried to resolve his own brokenness through violent anger. He spent many of his broken days imprisoning people who would not deny Jesus as he had. Many of the people he imprisoned were executed with his approval. Others were tortured.

Some of us try to resolve our own brokenness as Paul did through loud public actions that draw great attention to ourselves. Others may try to resolve brokenness as the woman at the well did, through the quiet lonely pursuit of invisibility where no one can see our shame and regret. No matter the method, all human attempts to resolve brokenness on our own just spiral us deeper and deeper into brokenness. The solution to our brokenness cannot come from the inside but must come from the outside. The solution to our brokenness requires a miracle from God. Brokenness as a result of sin is like death, an issue that can only be resolved by a miracle from God (Eph. 2:1-2).

CHOICE #2   *PAUL'S CHANGE*

Read Acts 26:12-20.

What were Jesus' instructions to Paul in verses 16-18? How did Paul respond in verses 19-20?

Do you think Jesus' instructions to Paul apply to you, too? How should you respond?

Paul had an incredible encounter with Jesus while traveling to Damascus. In his state of shock, the depths of Paul's heart were revealed. Paul referred to the blinding light and deafening voice as "Lord." He used this title because deep in his heart, Paul knew the story of Jesus was true. Paul knew he could not resolve his own brokenness. He needed Jesus.

Jesus' instructions to Paul were clear. He told Paul to repent and believe. Paul got up, repented of his sin, believed in Jesus, and offered hope to others.

God's instructions have not changed. He calls each of us to do the same. God calls each of us to repent of our sin and believe in Jesus for the restoration of our brokenness. Be courageous and respond as Paul did—get up, repent, and believe!

REPENT

The word for *repent* literally means to change one's mind. When God calls us to repent of our sin, He calls us to change our thinking about sin. He calls us to stop thinking sin is okay and agree that sin is wrong and deserving of death (Rom. 6:23). A change of mind leads to a change of heart that leads to a change in behavior.

BELIEVE

The word for *believe* literally means to trust, have faith, or believe to the point of complete trust. To believe is more than accepting a set of facts. To believe is more than affirming something or someone as true. To believe is to trust something or someone with your whole life. Biblical belief in Jesus is total trust in Him.

REALITY #3 | *THE GOSPEL RESCUED PAUL*

Read Acts 26:21-23.

What did the prophets and Moses say would take place according to verse 23?

Also based on verse 23, to whom is the gospel offered?

CHOICE #3 | *PAUL RECOVERED AND PURSUED GOD'S DESIGN*

Reread Acts 26:22.

What is the result of the gospel's work in Paul's life?

APPLY

If you have never made the initial decision to repent and believe, is there any reason you would not want to do that right now?

If you do make this decision today, be sure to tell a Christian friend or leader so they can help you with next steps?

Fill out this diagram with the three realities and three choices mentioned on page 7.

Find a partner and practice explaining the concepts of repentance and belief to him or her. Remember, a key word in the definition of repent is *change* and a key word in the definition of believe is *trust*.

GOD NEVER CHANGES HIS MIND

The average person makes many choices every day. These decisions include getting out of bed on time or hitting snooze one more time, who to sit with at lunch, whether to play video games or do homework, obey or disobey mom and dad, and so on. We all make thousands of choices, big and small, every day. How often do you change your mind?

Read Numbers 23:19. Based on this verse, fill in the blanks:

God will never _____.

God will never _____ His _____.

When God speaks, He will _____.

When God promises, He will _____.

God is not a man. He is not an angel. He is not any created being. God is a unique being, the only being who has always existed and always will.

God will never lie. As we think about our need to trust God, we can rest assured that every word He speaks is trustworthy. God's words never misalign with His actions. He will never promise something that He cannot or will not fulfill.

Lastly, God never changes His mind. Unlike us, God never chooses one option, then suddenly or slowly changes His mind to choose the other option. God has chosen to love you. God has chosen to call you to repentance and belief. God has chosen to return one day and make all things new. As we think about changing our mind to agree with God's view of sin, keep His unchanging mind in the background. It is not God's mind that needs to change, it is ours.

THE IMMUTABILITY OF GOD

Immutability is one of God's divine attributes. Other divine attributes of God include omniscience (all-knowing), omnipotence (all-powerful), omnipresence (all-present), sovereign (complete control), and holy (set apart). To be immutable is to always be the same. God is unchanging and unchangeable. His nature and His purposes will never change. Numbers 23:19 clearly points to this divine attribute of God. Other supporting verses are: Psalm 90:2; Malachi 3:6; Hebrews 13:8; and James 1:17.

Describe one promise that God has already fulfilled.

Describe one promise that God has yet to fulfill, but we trust that He will.

CHALLENGE OF THE DAY

Practice filling in the 3 Circles. When you get to the "repent & believe" arrow, stop and think about how God is calling you to change your mind.

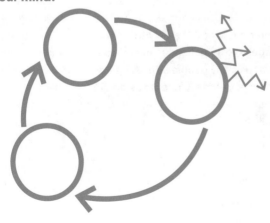

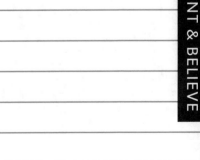

GOD IS WAITING FOR YOU

Every day we wait. We wait for the next episode to load on Netflix. We wait in a line of cars at a drive-thru for a hot sandwich, crisp fries, and a cold soda. We wait at red lights driving to and from school, church, or a friend's house. The average American spends approximately 58 hours waiting at red lights every year.[1] Did you know that God is waiting on you?

Read 2 Peter 3:9.

This verse tells us that God is waiting to fulfill His promise to come again. Why is God waiting?

God is in the business of making and keeping promises. He has already made and fulfilled thousands of clearly identifiable biblical promises. One of the promises God has yet to fulfill is His promise to come again and make all things new. Many Christians feel frustrated with God for taking so long to fulfill this promise. We want Him to come back and make everything right again. We believe He will, but we wonder when.

First, God does not think of time in the same way that we do. What feels like forever to us feels like a moment to God. Second, God has a really good reason for waiting. He has offered the world the only true solution to brokenness in the gospel and is patiently waiting to come again because He wants as many people as possible to repent and believe. God desires for as many people as possible to change their mind about sin, agree with His view of sin, and trust Christ with their whole life.

WAITING ON GOD

James 5:7-8 instructs Christians to wait patiently for Jesus to return. This is not easy. One of the things that makes this so hard is our prayers for physical healing. We may ask God to heal us, a family member, or a close friend. Sometimes, we do not experience healing this side of heaven. This can be sad, discouraging, and frustrating. This can cause us to beg God to return and wonder why He has not yet. It is encouraging to know God has not forgotten about us but has good reason for waiting to return. He desires as many people as possible to repent and believe in the gospel. It may be challenging at times, but keep waiting on God.

Describe something you've been waiting for God to do in your life.

God is patiently waiting for more people to repent. Name one person who you can share the gospel with while waiting on His return.

CHALLENGE OF THE DAY

Share the name of the person you just wrote above with one mentor (mom, dad, youth pastor, small group leader). Ask them to hold you accountable to share the 3 Circles with that person by the end of the week.

TRUST: THE WAY BACK TO GOD

We like to make sure that we give credit where credit is due —especially when that credit is due to us! We like to give and get credit for ideas and accomplishments. We might purchase things using credit cards. We know the movie is over when the credits start rolling. This idea of "credit" is commonplace in our everyday lives. The idea of credit is also throughout the Bible. In fact, credit has always been a key component of the way back to God.

Read Romans 4:3 (cf. Gen. 15:6).

Based on this verse, how did Abraham restore his relationship with God?

The common misconception is that Abraham restored his relationship with God by all of the good things that he did and animal sacrifices that he made. While Abraham did many good things and made many sacrifices, these actions are not what made him right with God. Abraham restored his relationship with God through belief. Abraham restored his relationship with God by trusting in His promises.

As a result of his belief, God credited His righteousness to Abraham. Abraham trusted the promises of God and God gave Abraham the gift of a restored relationship with Him. The way back to God has not changed. The way to restore our relationship with God is still trust. Only by believing in Him can we be credited righteousness. Only by trusting God with our whole life can we be given the gift of a restored relationship with Him.

IMPUTATION

The idea of imputation is a key theological term in the process of salvation. To impute is to credit an account or to transfer from one account to another. The moment that a person chooses to repent and believe the gospel, double imputation occurs simultaneously. The guilt of that person is imputed to Jesus and the righteousness of Jesus is imputed to that person. The moment a person chooses to repent and believe in the gospel, Jesus pays the full price for their sin. At the same time, that person takes on the full privileges of Christ's righteousness. When God looks at the repentant believer, He does not see the person's sin. Instead, when God looks at the repentant believer, He sees the righteousness of Jesus and is pleased with the restored relationship they may now enjoy.

Fill in the blanks:

The moment I repented and believed in the gospel, my _____ was credited to Jesus and His _____ was credited to me. When God looks at me, He does not see my _____, but instead sees the _____ of Jesus.

CHALLENGE OF THE DAY

Post something like the following on your favorite social media platform. No matter how you choose to word the post, be sure to use the #3Circles.

I made the choice to restore my relationship with God and I'm so glad I did! Want to know how? Ask me! #3Circles

THE GOSPEL

START

The gospel is the heart of this study. Everything up to this point has brought us here to the gospel. God's design points to the gospel. Our sin points to the gospel. Our brokenness points to the gospel. Our attempts to fix our brokenness point us to the gospel. Repentance and belief point to the gospel. So, what is the gospel?

> **How would you explain the gospel if someone asked? What are some key elements to the gospel? What makes it good news?**

The gospel is a Bible word that means "good news." The apostle Paul gives the most succinct biblical definition of the gospel in 1 Corinthians 15:1-4. The gospel is the good news that Jesus died on the cross for our sins, was buried, and God raised Him from the dead.

The gospel is central to the Christian life. The gospel is not only our way into the Christian life, but it is also the good news we need each day as we face trial after trial while walking through the Christian life. The gospel continually reminds us that we, in and of ourselves, are unable to fix the brokenness that we and others have caused. It reminds us that true and lasting change must come from outside of ourselves—from God Himself. That is the message of the gospel.

WATCH

Watch the video "The Gospel," before transitioning to the Discuss section.

DISCUSS

 REALITY #1 *GOD'S DESIGN FOR REDEMPTION*

Read Luke 23:26-27,32-56; 24:1-12.

In the garden of Eden, God revealed His plan to deal with sin. The first sin demanded the first sacrifice because the penalty for sin is death. God covered Adam and Eve's nakedness with animal skins. As the years went on, God required a system of sacrifices to cover the sins of His people. God allowed innocent animals who didn't have the ability to sin to die in the place of people who actually sinned. The blood of the animal paid the penalty for the person offering the sacrifice. The priest would use the animal's blood to signify that the person was forgiven because the animal died in their place.

Just as God allowed animals to be sacrificed for sin in the Old Testament, He allowed Jesus to be sacrificed for the sins of the world in the New Testament. God sent His Son, Jesus, who was innocent, to die in place of people who actually sinned. When someone repents and believes, they claim Jesus as their substitute because Jesus has died in their place.

CHOICE #1 *ALL HAVE SINNED*

The criminals in Luke 23 had committed crimes against society. They were caught, accused, tried, and sentenced to death. They paid the price the law required for their crimes. In our culture, when someone commits a crime and gets sent to prison, we say they are paying their debt to society. When we sin against God's law, we are committing crimes against God. When we sin, we owe a debt to God. In Luke 23:41, one of the criminals acknowledged his guilt because he knew he was a sinner. The Bible says that all have sinned. We know experientially that this is true. We fail to meet the demands of God's law. We have difficulty keeping the rules set for us by our parents, teachers, coaches, pastors, and others in authority over us. The truth is that we can't even keep the rules we make for ourselves. That's why when the Bible says that "all have sinned" (Rom. 3:23), we all have to acknowledge that this is true.

Do you find it easy or difficult to acknowledge your own sin and your own failures?

Do you agree that you have personally committed crimes against God's law?

REALITY #2   OUR BROKENNESS

It is difficult to find a better illustration of brokenness than a crucifixion. The entire ordeal was a painful and humiliating experience. The criminals in the story were being crucified for crimes they actually committed. The cross was a consequence for those crimes.

"The pain of crucifixion was absolutely unbearable," observes Dr. Alexander Metherell, PhD. "In fact, it was literally beyond words to describe; they had to invent a new word: excruciating. Literally, 'excruciating' means out of the cross."[1]

When we sin against God, we face consequences as well. Some of the consequences of sin can be physical and experiential. For example, if you lie to your parents, they lose trust in you to tell the truth. But there are also spiritual and eternal consequences for our sins. The Bible says that our sins actually create separation between us and God. The Bible says both physical and spiritual death are consequences of sin. Spiritual death is separation from God forever in hell.

You may or may not agree with the severity of their sentence, but does it seem fair to you that the criminals in the story had to pay a debt to society? Why or why not?

Does it make sense to you that people who have sinned against God owe a debt to Him? Explain.

CHOICE #2   IT'S NEVER TOO LATE TO REPENT & BELIEVE

The criminals in the story were literally hours or even minutes away from physical death. Under the pain and pressure of crucifixion, one criminal hardened his heart and died in his sin and his brokenness. The other criminal expressed repentance and confessed his own sins (v. 41). He believed in Jesus and asked Jesus to save him (v. 42). This guy could not do one thing to save himself. He could not do a single good work to make up for the bad things that he had done. He could not go to church. He could not be baptized. He could not give money to the poor. As he hung there—with his arms extended and the life bleeding out of him—literally, the only thing he could do was repent and believe—and he did.

Have you ever had the thought that a certain person or kind of a person is beyond forgiveness and redemption? Have you ever wondered if you have gone too far in your sins for God to forgive you?

JESUS EXCHANGES OUR SIN FOR HIS RIGHTEOUSNESS

When Jesus was hanging on the cross, God did a miracle. God took the sins of the world and placed them on Jesus. As Jesus was dying on the cross between the two criminals, He had the sin and the brokenness and the shame of the world hanging on the cross with Him. When someone repents and believes, God exchanges that person's sin for the righteousness of Jesus.

We have already established that because we are sinners, each one of us owes a debt to God. That sin-debt can only be paid through physical and spiritual death. When Jesus died on the cross, He paid that debt so that those who repent and believe can be spiritually debt-free. Because of what Jesus did on the cross, believers are forgiven for all of our sins.

How does the idea that you owe a sin-debt to God make you feel?

Have you repented and believed in Jesus to clear that debt forever?

What is most appealing to you about spending eternity in heaven?

CHOICE #3 **WE CAN RECOVER AND PURSUE GOD'S DESIGN**

It is obvious that every person has to die. The Bible promises believers a resurrection to everlasting life (John 5:29). When Jesus was raised from the dead in this story, He proved that He is the Son of God and that He has defeated sin and death. When He emerged from the grave, everyone had to acknowledge His supernatural standing as the Son of God. The resurrection of Jesus is the convincing evidence that God has the power to raise people from the dead. The resurrection of Jesus gives us assurance that we will be raised from the dead, just like Jesus.

When people explain the gospel, they almost always talk about the cross, but they often minimize or leave out the resurrection. The cross without the resurrection is not good news. The resurrection is part of what makes the story of the cross good news. The apostle Paul said that the cross and the resurrection are the most important things for people to believe and talk about.

CHRISTIAN RESURRECTION

Christians believe that they will be physically, bodily raised from the dead to live in heaven forever. While we might not know every detail, we can be certain that it will happen.

How is the Christian view of the resurrection different from other views of the afterlife?

Does the resurrection of Jesus make you personally more confident about what will happen to you after you die?

APPLY

How does the gospel bring you hope? What circles of influence has God given you to share the good news of the gospel?

Fill out this diagram with the three realities and three choices mentioned on page 7.

Find a friend or partner and practice explaining the gospel to him or her (Remember: the gospel is that Jesus died on the cross for our sins, He was buried, and God raised Him from the dead.).

WHAT IS THE GOSPEL?

There are certain words in the English language that are commonly used but difficult to define. Words like "love" or "literally" or "epic" all have a variety of meanings. Some even say that the definition of insanity is doing the same thing and expecting different results, but that's not actually the definition of insanity.[2] We have lost a basic understanding of some words. A Bible word that seems to have lost its meaning is the word "gospel."

Ask someone "What is the gospel?" and you will get a variety of responses. Some will say, "It's a genre of music." Still others would guess, "It's a way to express something is really true." Others might say, "It's the first four books of the New Testament that describe the life of Jesus." So, what is "the gospel" according to the Bible?

Read 1 Corinthians 15:1-8.

The apostle Paul declared that the gospel is of the highest importance. He then listed each component of this "most important message." Jesus died for your sins in fulfillment of the Old Testament scriptures, He was buried, and He rose again on the third day. He then appeared to many witnesses in His resurrected state. This is the gospel.

What makes this message so important? It has power. It changes lives. It includes all people. It's how we are saved from all of our sin—past, present, and future—for all of eternity! Paul reminds us that the gospel allows us to live according to God's design. The gospel is more than a one-time decision. The gospel calls us to a new way of living.

Have you ever had the opportunity to visit an escape room? There are different themes, challenges, and levels of difficulty, but they all have similar objectives. The group is in a locked room and has to work together to find clues. The clues lead you to keys that eventually unlock the door which allows you to escape the room. Most places give you 60 minutes to escape. It can be extremely frustrating or extremely rewarding. The difference in the experience hinges on the group's ability to work together in order to find clues that lead to freedom. Paul is at the end of the "60 minutes." He's got the group's attention and is giving them the key to escape brokenness. The most difficult part has been done for you. All you need to do is take the key and open the door.

Have you ever trusted the gospel message to rescue you from your sins?

When did you make that decision?

If not, what is keeping you from making the decision to repent and believe?

CHALLENGE OF THE DAY

Discuss today's devotional with one mentor (mom, dad, youth pastor, or small group leader). Tell them if you made a decision to believe today or tell them the correct definition of the gospel according to 1 Corinthians 15:3-4.

THE GOSPEL

THE GREATEST GIFT

Take a minute to think about one of the best gifts you've ever received. Was it a possession? An experience? A thoughtful gesture? Draw a picture, a symbol, or sketch word art below that reminds you of that gift.

Who did it come from? Why did it mean so much to you at the time?

John 3:16 is arguably the most well-known Bible verse of all time. It's on store fronts, billboards, bumper stickers, social media bios, and on posters at major sporting events. Why does this verse get so much attention? Perhaps because it's describing the greatest gift given by the greatest gift giver to the greatest number of people. Let's look at each of these details and see how they relate to us personally.

Read John 3:16-21.

Who is the gift giver? _____

What is the gift? _____

Who is the gift for? _____

The giver is God the Father. He is the God of the universe—the Creator of heaven and earth. He knitted you together in your mother's womb. God knows you. He loves you. God provides for and sustains you. As a good Father, God understands the greatest needs of His children.

The gift is God's one and only Son, Jesus, and an eternity spent in His presence. The Bible calls it heaven. Since sin entered the world, God knew mankind's greatest need was to restore our relationship to Him. The only avenue for that to happen would be through a perfect sacrifice. Jesus was the perfect sacrifice. The gift of Jesus is offered to every person in the world.

If you have received Jesus by faith, take a moment to thank God for His incredible gift.

CHALLENGE OF THE DAY

Offer God's greatest gift to others today by posting John 3:16 on social media with #3Circles.

CHANGE WITH AN EXCHANGE

Think back to your life seven years ago. If you can, pull up a picture of yourself.

How old were you? _____

List the differences from then to now. Appearance, responsibilities, relationships, thoughts, and so on.

What changes have occurred in your life over the last seven years?

Read 2 Corinthians 5:16-21. Underline verse 17.

God gives us a new identity.

2 Corinthians 5:17 says that anyone who is in Christ is a _____ _____.

Paul often uses the phrase "in Christ" to describe this new identity. You are a child of God once and for all. This change is only possible because of the exchange of your sin for Jesus' righteousness. Jesus paid the debt you owed by paying the ultimate sacrifice. You exchanged your sin for His righteousness and now you are reconciled to God.

God gives us a new position. 2 Corinthians 5:21 says we are _____ for Christ.

An ambassador is an official representative from one country to another country. Ambassadors are given the authority to speak on behalf of the country that they are representing. This position is often given to well-respected, accomplished people who remain loyal to their country.

Likewise, God is counting on us to be His ambassadors who speak on His behalf to others. He wants us to appeal to others to be made right with God. We need to tell them that God has made a way for people to step out of brokenness and recover and pursue His design. All they have to do is repent and believe the gospel.

The good news is that Jesus died on the cross for our sins, was buried, and God raised Him from the dead.

Place a check by the places where you currently serve as an ambassador or add your own places:

☐ **Home**   ☐ **Work**

☐ **School**   ☐ **Church**

☐ **Sports**   ☐ **Neighborhood**

☐ **Team**

CHALLENGE OF THE DAY

Who has God placed in your life who needs to hear the gospel message? Pray this name out loud.

Ask God to give you the boldness to be His ambassador and use the 3 Circles to deliver this message.

Practice here:

RECOVER & PURSUE

START

Everyone loves a do-over. When you were a kid and you completely botched a kick in a game of backyard kickball, you asked your friends for a do-over. When you forget your lines in the school play, you can't wait to redeem yourself in the next performance. When you fail a test, you can only hope the teacher will have mercy and give you another shot at it. When we sin, we are thankful God offers us do-over after do-over. This is what it means to recover and pursue God's design.

We talked a lot about the gospel last session. We saw how God exchanges the sin of all who repent and believe in Jesus for all of Jesus' righteousness. Our heart-decision and mouth-confession put us in right-standing with God (Rom. 10:9-10) and the Holy Spirit seals the deal (Eph. 1:13). The Holy Spirit is who motivates us to live life according to God's design. We still have to fight our sin nature and our tendency to violate God's design. We fall, but we get back up with the help of the Holy Spirit and our church family. The Holy Spirit is always there to help us recover and pursue God's design.

When is the last time you made a mistake and asked someone for a do-over?

Were you able to redeem yourself the second time? What about the third time?

WATCH

Watch the video "Recover and Pursue," before transitioning to the Discuss section.

DISCUSS

GOD'S DESIGN FOR PETER

The apostle Peter knew what it was like to need a lot of do-overs. Peter knew what it was like to fall and get back up again. After spending three years as a disciple of Jesus, watching Jesus do miracles and listening to His teaching, you would think that Peter would prove to be a loyal friend. But when Jesus was arrested, Peter betrayed their friendship and denied even knowing Jesus at all. Peter messed up badly and Jesus graciously restored him. Peter then went on to recover and pursue God's design for his life.

Read John 1:35-37,40-42.

The name Cephas/Peter means rock. Peter was among the first to follow Jesus. Jesus knew Peter inside and out. He knew all of Peter's strengths and all of his weaknesses. He knew that Peter would stumble, fall, and get back up again. Jesus knew that Peter would believe and keep on believing. This is why Jesus told Peter that his faith was the rock on whom Jesus would build His church. God had a design for Peter.

Why would "faith like a rock" be important for Peter's future?

CHOICE #1 *PETER DENIED JESUS*

Read Luke 22:54-62.

Peter denied knowing Jesus—not once, not twice, but three times. Each time he said it, Peter got more and more emphatic.

Why do you think Peter denied knowing Jesus?

Have you ever been reluctant to tell someone that you are a follower of Jesus? What emotions motivated your reluctance?

REALITY #2 *PETER'S BROKENNESS*

Reread Luke 22:61-62.

Imagine what it must have felt like for Peter to look across the courtyard and see Jesus looking at him in that moment. We have no way of knowing what look was on Jesus' face. Many people have speculated it was a look of compassion because we know it is God's kindness that leads us to repentance (Rom. 2:4). Peter's heart broke over his sin. He left the courtyard and "wept bitterly."

Imagine what it would be like to have Jesus walk in on you if you lied to your mom, if you cheated on a test, or if you looked at pornography on your phone. Imagine His eyes catching yours and holding them for a moment. Imagine the mix of hurt, disappointment, love, and compassion.

Do you think you would react the same way that Peter did? Why or why not?

CHOICE #2   PETER REPENTED

Peter's tears demonstrate sorrow for sin. We know from reading the Gospels that he remained committed to the other disciples even after his humiliating experiences. After Jesus rose from the dead, Peter sought Jesus out. He ran to the tomb when he heard that Jesus had been raised from the dead (John 20:2-4). He jumped out of the boat and swam to the shore when he saw Jesus standing on the banks of the Sea of Galilee (John 21:7). Peter knew that he had sinned, but he also believed that Jesus would forgive him. He was eager to be restored by Jesus so he could pursue the mission that Jesus was going to give him.

REALITY #3   JESUS FORGAVE & RESTORED PETER

Read John 21:15-17.

This is one of the most dramatic stories of forgiveness and restoration in the Bible. Jesus went to find Peter. Then He cooked Peter a meal and engaged Peter in a conversation and asked Peter if he loved Him. Peter got to tell Jesus that he loved Him not once, not twice, but three times. This story presents a powerful picture of complete and total restoration and forgiveness.

When have you ever really messed up and been forgiven?

How has someone restored you when you didn't deserve it?

Read Acts 2:36-41.

Just weeks after his greatest failure, Peter preached his most powerful sermon. On that day, 3,000 people believed the gospel because of Peter's preaching.

When Jesus forgave Peter, He didn't ask Peter to go back and change his past. Jesus didn't even change his past. Jesus forgave his past and He redeemed his past. Redeem in this sense means to take something that is bad and turn it around for good. God didn't erase Peter's betrayal, but God used Peter's sinful experience to change Peter for the better. We can be sure that Peter never forgot the night he betrayed Jesus, nor the morning when Jesus restored him.

When you become a Christian, God doesn't erase your past. The consequences for your sins are still there. The habits you have developed may not automatically go away. The wounds you carry because of sins that others committed against you are not instantly healed. That is not how the gospel works. There are some situations that are so broken and some wounds that are so deep they will not be healed until we get to heaven.

While your past is not erased, the gospel will make your life different. When Jesus comes into your life, He gives you the Holy Spirit who begins to teach you how to think, feel, respond, and how to live in the way that Jesus wants you to. In addition to receiving the Holy Spirit, a new believer is also joined to a new family–the family of God. This is why it's so important for new believers to be baptized and become a part of a church. A church is the expression of God's family on earth. A church is there to encourage us, help us, and teach us. When we fall down, the Holy Spirit and our church family help us get back up. Believers can recover and pursue God's design.

After Jesus restored Peter, he became a great preacher, a bold leader, and a powerful ambassador for the gospel. He wrote at least two books of the Bible. He is one of the most recognizable characters in the New Testament. There are cities and churches named after him literally all over the world. Peter's influence continues to this day even though he's been dead for 2,000 years. Despite his famous failures, Peter was restored. God allowed him to recover and pursue His design for his life. God will do for you what he did for Peter.

Do you think Peter's story is a one-of-a-kind story? Why or why not?

APPLY

What are some areas that you have been able to recover and pursue God's design in your own life?

Fill out this diagram with the three realities and three choices mentioned on page 7.

Find a partner or friend and practice explaining what it means to recover and pursue God's design.

THE COMEBACK

Comeback stories are powerful. Before he built the world's most visited theme park, Walt Disney's first company went bankrupt. He was also fired from a Missouri newspaper for "not being creative enough." Today The Walt Disney Company is worth an estimated $130 billion.[1]

One of the lessons that a parent has to teach a child is to get up with they fall down. A parent that does everything for a child actually hurts the child because that child won't learn to do anything for themselves. One of the best lessons you can learn in life is that when you fall down, you get back up. That's what redemption is all about. When someone fails in life, many people will push them down and push them out. Sometimes even Christians will be judgmental, harsh, and mean-spirited when they see someone involved in sinful, immoral, or unethical behavior. This is unfortunate because Jesus was called a friend of sinners. Jesus does not push people down and push them out—Jesus pulls people in and lifts them up.

Read John 8:2-11.

In this story, the Pharisees humiliated this woman who had been caught sleeping with a man she was not married to.

The Pharisees expected Jesus to condemn the woman, but He didn't. Instead He forgave her. But what was Jesus' final command to the woman?

Jesus took someone who was guilty of sin, forgave her, restored her, and encouraged her to recover and pursue God's design for her life.

Have you ever been involved in sinful behavior that hurt your reputation because it became public knowledge? How did that make you feel?

74 | 3 CIRCLES

Have you ever committed a sin that seemed so severe you were afraid if other people found out, they would never allow you to be restored? What did you do?

Have you ever committed the same sin over and over again and wondered if God will still forgive you and restore you? Why do you think people sometimes feel this way?

How does the story in John 8 relate to the questions above?

CHALLENGE OF THE DAY

Practice filling in the 3 Circles (refer to page 7).

What are some areas where you need to begin pursuing God's design for your life? Pray and ask Him to help you.

FROM ORDINARY TO EXTRAORDINARY

He's just an ordinary looking guy with horned-rim glasses until he steps into the phone booth. Then he steps out dressed in blue tights and red cape, thrusts his fist into the air, and flies away. It's not a bird. It's not a plane. It's Superman—the leader of the Justice League. Perhaps this is the sense people got when they met Peter after Jesus was resurrected from the dead.

Read Acts 4:13.

Peter's background was not impressive and yet something about him caught the attention of the most prominent religious people in Jerusalem. It was only days earlier that Peter denied knowing Jesus to a little girl and now Peter is speaking boldly about Jesus in front of hostile crowds. Peter had fallen down, but he got back up with the help of the Holy Spirit. When you look you back to Acts 2, you see that it wasn't the phone booth that transformed Peter. He was transformed by a powerful prayer meeting and a fiery encounter with the Holy Spirit.

Read Acts 2:1-4.

> Circle the first nine words in verse 4.
>
> Peter was filled with the _____
> _____ and that's what made all of
> the difference.

Jesus had told the disciples that the Holy Spirit would give them power. The Spirit gave Peter the power he needed to recover and pursue God's design. This same superpower belongs to all who repent and believe in Jesus.

The Holy Spirit comes into your life when you believe. He gives you the power to recover and pursue God's design. He gives you the courage to talk about Jesus even when it seems like a risky thing to do.

Peter and the disciples were not immune to fear or intimidation. But they prayed constantly for courage and the Holy Spirit gave them what they needed. Consider this prayer from Acts 4 when the disciples were threatened with jail for speaking about Jesus:

Read Acts 4:29.

> **They prayed and asked God to help them speak His word with all _____.**

We can't live the Christian life on our own. We need the power of the Holy Spirit and we need to ask God to give us the boldness we lack.

CHALLENGE OF THE DAY

> **Take a moment and write a prayer yielding to the power of the Holy Spirit living in you asking Him to help you recover and pursue God's design:**
>
> _____
>
> _____
>
> _____
>
> _____
>
> _____

Now pray and ask the Holy Spirit to give you boldness to share the 3 Circles with someone you know who is still living in brokenness.

> **Write the person's name here:**
>
> _____

FIND A BAND OF BROTHERS AND SISTERS

The "Easy" Company of the United States Army's 101st Airborne Division helped end World War II. Author Stephen E. Ambrose made them famous as the Band of Brothers.[2] These were men fighting for their country and for one another. They trained together, fought together, bled together, and some of them died together. When one of them got injured, they rejoined their band of brothers on the front lines as soon as they could. This is a picture of what it sometimes feels like to be a Christian in today's world. We live in a world that sometimes seems to be warring against us. It's not easy to keep fighting. We need a band of brothers and sisters. We need people who can help us keep on recovering and keep on pursuing God's design.

Read Galatians 6:1-5.

Paul wrote these verses to a church in the city of Galatia. The church was full of people who had been transformed by the gospel. Unfortunately, many of the Christians in the church were struggling with sin. Paul reminded them that their church family was there so that they would help one another recover and pursue God's design.

Christianity is like a team sport. When someone on the team falls down, you help them get back up. We are called to be on the same squad. We need to do whatever we can to see each other win. We need to band together, trust in the gospel together, and do our best to point one another toward God's design. If sin takes one of us out, we do our best to restore one another with gentleness and respect.

Why shouldn't Christians be judgmental when other Christians fall into sin?

Have you ever had someone in your church family help you get back up? Who?

Who is in your band of brothers and sisters that can help you recover and pursue God's design?

CHALLENGE OF THE DAY

Take a picture with someone who is in your band of brothers and sisters and post it on your social media with #3Circles. You could say something like, "Thanks for helping me recover and pursue God's design for my life."

START

Use this introduction as a way to begin your group time before watching the session video.

WATCH

Watch the video for Session 1 (included in the DVD Kit). Allow students time to ask any clarifying questions about the video before continuing to the Discuss section using the content provided.

DISCUSS

Use the Discuss pages to guide your group through an in-depth discussion of the relevant biblical passages for this session. Adding to the video content, the Discuss section will provide additional insight and clarification into key biblical concepts as students work through the session content.

ACTIVITY

If you have a group of younger students, consider using this activity to illustrate the point that God's design is good and best for our lives. For the activity, you will need:

- At least one Lego set specific to build something, preferably with the box and instructions.
- At least one set of "free" Legos with no instructions or specific thing to build.

Give one group of students the Lego sets designed to build specific items. Give another group the "free" Legos. Give them some time and have them build their items.

Chances are, the students with specific instructions and sets will build something "cooler" than the kids with the free Legos. Talk about how these guys built something neater because they had a specific design to follow, with instructions, and so their Lego set ended up with more purpose than the other. Likewise, God's design in the world and in our lives is the best for us, giving us purpose and meaning as we live out His good design.

For the kids with the free Legos, you can talk about how God gave them an innate desire to design and create something cool. Even without a specific set of instructions, they still tried to design something that made sense and looked good.

LEADER GUIDE

APPLY

As a group or as individuals, work through the application section that follows the Discuss section. The Apply section provides an opportunity for students to master the material they just learned by engaging with the 3 Circles diagram. This can be accomplished as a group or have students break up into smaller groups to practice their dialogue using the 3 Circles.

PERSONAL STUDY

Introduce the Personal Study that follows the Apply section of the material to your students. Challenge and encourage them to read through the three studies provided before the next meeting.

NOTES

SESSION ONE

GOD'S DESIGN

START

Use this introduction as a way to begin your group time before watching the session video.

WATCH

Watch the video for Session 2 (included in the DVD Kit). Allow students time to ask any clarifying questions about the video before continuing to the Discuss section using the content provided.

DISCUSS

Use the Discuss pages to guide your group through an in-depth discussion of the relevant biblical passages for this session. Adding to the video content, the Discuss section will provide additional insight and clarification into key biblical concepts as students work through the session content.

> ### ACTIVITY
>
> If you have a group of younger students, consider using this activity to illustrate the point of sin and how we might fail to confess our sin.
>
> Share with students that they've been approached to write a book entitled, "The Middle School Student's Guide on How to Get Out of Trouble."
>
> They should first come up with a list of categories of different kinds of trouble middle schoolers get into: trouble with friends, school troubles, troubles with their sports team, trouble with their parents, and so on. Each category should become a chapter of the book.
>
> Next, group students into smaller groups and assign each group a chapter. They should make a brief outline of how to get out of the particular kind of trouble they've been assigned.
>
> Ask them to share the ideas they came up with for each category. What approach did they generally take? Did anyone suggest confessing to the trouble, apologizing, and repenting? Talk about how we rarely confess to our sin, but rather compound it by adding more sin to try to cover up our sin (e.g., cheating on a test but then lying about it; spreading gossip about a friend but then ignoring that friend instead of apologizing). Conclude by drawing parallels to the wrong approach David initially took with his sin and how he compounded it by trying to cover it up.

LEADER GUIDE

APPLY

As a group or as individuals, work through the application section that follows the Discuss section. The Apply section provides an opportunity for students to master the material they just learned by engaging with the 3 Circles diagram. This can be accomplished as a group or have students break up into smaller groups to practice their dialogue using the 3 Circles.

PERSONAL STUDY

Introduce the Personal Study that follows the Apply section of the material to your students. Challenge and encourage them to read through the three studies provided before the next meeting.

NOTES

SESSION TWO

SIN

START

Use this introduction as a way to begin your group time before watching the session video.

WATCH

Watch the video for Session 3 (included in the DVD Kit). Allow students time to ask any clarifying questions about the video before continuing to the Discuss section using the content provided.

DISCUSS

Use the Discuss pages to guide your group through an in-depth discussion of the relevant biblical passages for this session. Adding to the video content, the Discuss section will provide additional insight and clarification into key biblical concepts as students work through the session content.

ACTIVITY

If you have a group of younger students, consider using this activity to illustrate the point of how humanity was designed for relationships, but because of sin, those relationships have been broken. Before the class, make a list of things that come in pairs or often go together. Some examples:

- Peanut butter and jelly
- Burger and fries
- Bread and butter

- Mario and Luigi
- Bacon and eggs
- Batman and Robin

- Han Solo and Chewie
- (a pair of) scissors
- (a pair of) pants

Play charades with your list, but instruct students to go up two at a time (e.g., two kids have to try to act out Batman and Robin, or two kids try to act out bacon and eggs).

Once the kids are through your list, see if they can figure out the pattern: everything is a pair; they all relate! You can ask the kids how the game would have been different (i.e., harder) if they had to do the charades by themselves.

Explain that the point of the activity was to show that relationships help. In addition, explain that many great things come in relationships. Ask them how hard it would be for one hand to clap, or one lip to whistle, or to have a sandwich with only one piece of bread (not folded in half). In a similar way, we were created for relationships with God, with one another, and with the world! However, because of sin, those relationships have become fractured and in need of repair.

LEADER GUIDE

APPLY

As a group or as individuals, work through the application section that follows the Discuss section. The Apply section provides an opportunity for students to master the material they just learned by engaging with the 3 Circles diagram. This can be accomplished as a group or have students break up into smaller groups to practice their dialogue using the 3 Circles.

PERSONAL STUDY

Introduce the Personal Study that follows the Apply section of the material to your students. Challenge and encourage them to read through the three studies provided before the next meeting.

SESSION THREE

BROKENNESS

START

Use this introduction as a way to begin your group time before watching the session video.

WATCH

Watch the video for Session 4 (included in the DVD Kit). Allow students time to ask any clarifying questions about the video before continuing to the Discuss section using the content provided.

DISCUSS

Use the Discuss pages to guide your group through an in-depth discussion of the relevant biblical passages for this session. Adding to the video content, the Discuss section will provide additional insight and clarification into key biblical concepts as students work through the session content.

ACTIVITY

If you have a group of younger students, consider using this activity to illustrate the point of the lesson on repentance.

To begin, ask the students to come up with a list of places. They can be everyday locations such as a convenience store, or way out there such as District 11 from *The Hunger Games*.

Break students into groups, and instruct each group to pick one of the places. Now, the students have to make a parable set in the place they picked. The parable must show the difference between mere remorse (regret for circumstances) and true repentance (a genuine change of heart).

Give them time to prep, then have them present. Hopefully, their settings will spur them to some unique ideas on demonstrating mere remorse and full repentance. Correct what needs correcting, and celebrate what they did well. Debrief by pointing out that true repentance begins with the mind and heart and leads toward the action of turning away from sin and turning toward Christ for forgiveness.

LEADER GUIDE

APPLY

As a group or as individuals, work through the application section that follows the Discuss section. The Apply section provides an opportunity for students to master the material they just learned by engaging with the 3 Circles diagram. This can be accomplished as a group or have students break up into smaller groups to practice their dialogue using the 3 Circles.

PERSONAL STUDY

Introduce the Personal Study that follows the Apply section of the material to your students. Challenge and encourage them to read through the three studies provided before the next meeting.

NOTES

SESSION FOUR

REPENT
& BELIEVE

START

Use this introduction as a way to begin your group time before watching the session video.

WATCH

Watch the video for Session 5 (included in the DVD Kit). Allow students time to ask any clarifying questions about the video before continuing to the Discuss section using the content provided.

DISCUSS

Use the Discuss pages to guide your group through an in-depth discussion of the relevant biblical passages for this session. Adding to the video content, the Discuss section will provide additional insight and clarification into key biblical concepts as students work through the session content.

ACTIVITY

If you have a group of younger students, consider using this activity to illustrate the essential elements of the gospel.

To begin, break your students into smaller groups. Explain that they are investigative journalist teams. Their job is present a short documentary or news story on who Jesus of Nazareth is and what the gospel is about. They should try to be as thorough as possible, using the gospel accounts and other historical evidence available.

Give them time to prep and then to present their newscasts or documentaries (if they need hints on what to put in their skits, they could do interviews, read quotes, have one student act as a reporter at the scene of the action, and so on.).

Once they've finished, debrief how they did. Did they get the essentials? How did they define the gospel? Who did they say Jesus is? Use this as a way to supplement the session material on what the gospel is about.

APPLY

As a group or as individuals, work through the application section that follows the Discuss section. The Apply section provides an opportunity for students to master the material they just learned by engaging with the 3 Circles diagram. This can be accomplished as a group or have students break up into smaller groups to practice their dialogue using the 3 Circles.

PERSONAL STUDY

Introduce the Personal Study that follows the Apply section of the material to your students. Challenge and encourage them to read through the three studies provided before the next meeting.

NOTES

SESSION FIVE

THE GOSPEL

START

Use this introduction as a way to begin your group time before watching the session video.

WATCH

Watch the video for Session 6 (included in the DVD Kit). Allow students time to ask any clarifying questions about the video before continuing to the Discuss section using the content provided.

DISCUSS

Use the Discuss pages to guide your group through an in-depth discussion of the relevant biblical passages for this session. Adding to the video content, the Discuss section will provide additional insight and clarification into key biblical concepts as students work through the session content.

ACTIVITY

If you have a group of younger students, consider using this activity as a wrap up to the final session.

Ask students to imagine that some local school districts have hired your group out to make some posters they have to put up in their halls. The posters are to line up with the *3 Circles* framework. Specifically, they want a poster designed for each circle:

- The first poster should focus on the first circle, having both the design and summary of what the first circle represents.
- The second poster should focus on the second circle, having both the design and summary of what the second circle represents.
- The third poster should focus on the third circle, having both the design and summary of what the third circle represents.

Some of the districts are public schools and some are Christian, so your kids can make posters that would benefit both groups that read them. They can incorporate any illustrations they remember throughout the study or come up with original ones for themselves. Feel free to split the students up as you see best: as individuals or as groups; you can assign a group of three posters to a single group, or one poster per group. Let the students present their posters, allowing them the opportunity to walk through the 3 Circles framework in front of their peers.

LEADER GUIDE

APPLY

As a group or as individuals, work through the application section that follows the Discuss section. The Apply section provides an opportunity for students to master the material they just learned by engaging with the 3 Circles diagram. This can be accomplished as a group or have students break up into smaller groups to practice their dialogue using the 3 Circles.

PERSONAL STUDY

Introduce the Personal Study that follows the Apply section of the material to your students. Challenge and encourage them to read through the three studies provided before the next meeting.

NOTES

SESSION SIX

RECOVER & PURSUE

SESSION 1

1. *Chariots of Fire*, directed by Hugh Hudson (1981; England, UK: Twentieth Century Fox, DVD, 1982). (p. 15 of our study)

2. *Toy Story 4,* directed by Josh Cooley (2019; Emeryville, CA: Pixar Animation Studios & Walt Disney Pictures, DVD, 2019).

SESSION 2

1. Walvoord, John F., and Roy B. Zuck. *Bible Knowledge Commentary* (Dallas, TX: Victor Books, 1985), 467.

2. "Calculation Error? Math Majors Send Massive Snowball Rolling into Dorm," CBS News, February 14, 2014, https://www.cbsnews.com/news/runaway-snowball-slams-into-reed-college-dorm-in-portland-oregon/.

SESSION 3

1. "The Cracked Pot: A Story for Anyone Who's Not Quite Perfect," Amazing Women Rock, accessed on January 21, 2020, https://amazingwomenrock.com/the-story-of-the-cracked-pot-for-anyone-whos-not-quite-perfect.

SESSION 4

1. Sarah Crow, "You'll Spend Much of Your Life Waiting at Red Lights," Best Life, September 19, 2018, https://bestlifeonline.com/red-lights/.

SOURCES

SESSION 5

1. Sheri Bell, "Crucifixion Details of the Resurrection of Christ," Josh McDowell Ministry, March 8, 2017, https://www.josh.org/resurrection-crucifixion-details/?mwm_id=241874010218&mot=J79GNF&gclid=CjwKCAiAwZTuBRAY EiwAcr67OSA_bgBhLbe9QC69qGMQtn7JZbUXnYNJfl6RSEms8gONIlKSC8 PPWRoCSWkQAvD_BwE.

SESSION 6

1. Hillary Hoffower, "A Fued Over a $400 Million Trust Fund, a Massive Fortune that Left One Heiress with an Inferiority Complex, and a Sprawling Media Empire. Meet the Disney family," Business Insider, June 10,2019, https://www.businessinsider.com/disney-family-net-worth-fortune-media-walt-2019-6.

2. "World War II Hero from Band of Brothers Dies," History.com, last modified August 29,2018, https://www.history.com/news/world-war-ii-hero-from-band-of-brothers-dies.

NOTES